Orthodoxy for Children

Vladimir Luchaninov

The Divine Liturgy

**Illustrations by
Anastasia Novik**

Grand Rapids · Exaltation Press · 2020

Copyright © 2020 Exaltation Press

Author: Vladimir Luchaninov
Illustrator: Anastasia Novik
Translator: Fr. John Hogg

"The Divine Liturgy"
      This book is designed to help children understand the purpose of fasting in the Orthodox Church. It begins by talking about the difference between dieting for health reasons and fasting for God. It then looks at the Church calendar, noting when and why we fast, and explaining what is more important than food in order to fast in a God-pleasing way.

All rights reserved. This book or any portion thereof may not be reproduced or used in any manner whatsoever without the express written permission of the publisher except for the use of brief quotations in a book review.

Translated from the original "О Постах" by Nikea Press, Copyright © Trading house «NIKEA», www.Nikeabooks.ru

ISBN: 978-1-950067-37-4 (Hardcover)

Edited by Cynthia Hogg
Graphical editing by Emily Harju

First printing edition 2020

Exaltation Press
Grand Rapids, MI

www.ExaltationPress.com

For bulk orders, please contact editor@exaltationpress.com.

Table of Contents

SEEING WITH THE HEART 4
A CONVERSATION WITH GOD 6
A COMMON WORK 8
GOD LOVES US 10
PREPARATION 14
IN THE KINGDOM OF GOD 18
THE LITURGY AND THE WHOLE WORLD 20
THE HOLY GOSPEL 22
THE GREAT ENTRANCE 24
THE HEART OF LITURGY 26
THE LORD IS WAITING FOR YOU 30
AN EXPLANATION OF TWO IMPORTANT PRAYERS 32

SEEING WITH THE HEART

You're getting ready to go to Church or more likely, your parents have woken you up and while you're still sleepy, they're getting you ready. You are going to Liturgy. Many people sleep in on Sunday for as long as they can, but you know that a few extra hours spent in bed will not really bring happiness. Soon, you will be in a world of wonder where a miracle will take place, a true miracle. You've dreamed about that, haven't you? During Liturgy, you can boldly ask Jesus Christ for all your needs. Only don't doubt! Liturgy is the best time for a miracle.

"But at Liturgy there are so many adults that all I see is their legs and backs! How can I ask Christ for what I need if I can't even see Him? And if I do see Him, it's just in the icons and you can't really talk to an icon the way you can talk to other people in Church!"

That's an important question so let's work through it. We can see with our eyes. That's easy, especially if our vision is good. However, we can also see with our hearts and that's something we have to learn.

How do you learn, for example, to draw? By making an effort. The more we practice, the better we get at it. The same thing is true about our ability to see with our hearts. That ability has been placed inside us but we just need to bring it out. Sometimes it takes us our whole lives to learn how but that isn't bad, to spend our whole lives learning. It's like going to a party. The way itself is joyful because we're not just going anywhere, but to a party.

The Divine Liturgy

The church temple is sometimes called the House of God on Earth.

Lampadas glimmer in front of the icons and people light candles as they quietly pray for their needs. The icons are marvelous images. As we gaze on the faces of God, the Theotokos, the angels, and the saints, we can talk to them and little by little, we begin to see and hear them with our hearts.

A CONVERSATION WITH GOD

Those adults in front of you in Church on Sunday came for a reason. They came to see God with their hearts and to talk with Him. Talking to God is called "prayer." You may not yet understand all the prayers that you hear in Church but with time, you will come to understand them. Listen closely, ask adults, but most importantly, begin yourself to talk with God in simple words.

It's important to learn how to understand God's answers. You won't hear them with your ears. His answers might come through other people, through things that happen unexpectedly, or through a miracle. Learn not only to see but also to hear with your heart. And make sure that all of your desires are for what is good!

When we come to Liturgy, we bring our good desires to our good Master, Jesus Christ. The saints and people who lived hundreds and even thousands of years before us come to Liturgy with us because those who see Jesus Christ with their hearts never die. Their souls live in eternal joy in the Kingdom of God.

Did you know you can pray to God for anything? For example:

"Lord, I believe and know that you hear me. My parents don't want a kitten but I really do! Please give us a kitten but also make it so that the kitten brings mom and dad joy and doesn't make things harder for them!"

The Temple

In the Orthodox Church, the physical Church buildings in which we worship are often called "temples," because they are places dedicated to the worship of God. They are also called "houses," because they are the house of God. If we are members of His family through Holy Baptism, His house is our house, too!

A COMMON WORK

We gather together for Liturgy to give thanks to God for our life. During Liturgy, you do many things. You look around you and see the beauty of God's world, you think, you move from place to place, and smile and laugh as you encounter your favorite tastes and smells. Each time, you learn something new. How wonderful that is!

Sometimes, we can get used to life and it can feel boring. "Life is the same as always," we think. "What's so special about my life?" Only after an illness, when we finally feel better, do we realize how little we actually need to be happy: breathing fresh air, eating, smiling, spending time with our friends, and reading our favorite books.

Ungrateful people never see miracles because they always want more and always greedily look for something beyond what they already have.

Grateful people, however, value what they have and see the good that they have been given. Those are the kind of people who come to Liturgy to tell God "thank you" for the life He has given them. After all, life itself is a true miracle!

Thanksgiving

We all gather in Church together since Liturgy is our common work. That's what the Greek word "liturgy" means. We also call it the "Eucharist" (and it's okay if you don't memorize that right away). That means "thanksgiving." And thanksgiving is a word worth remembering!

9 The Divine Liturgy

Give thanks to God. Don't be shy about asking God your questions and even asking for things. For God, no concern is too little. He is attentive, generous, and loves doing what is good.

GOD LOVES US

The Lord often gave us the rules leading to eternal life but more often than not, we didn't follow them. The world around us exists according to its own rules. Some of those rules are visible. If you touch fire, you will definitely burn your hand. But there are also invisible rules. When we do something that's evil, we burn our souls. You don't notice it right away. Each time, however, the burn grows and over time, our souls are no longer able to do what is good. They grow dark and hardened, charred by sin, and deprived of eternal life.

In order to save us from perishing, God became man and entered the world. The Holy Spirit overshadowed the most tenderhearted of all the girls on earth, Mary, who would later be called the Theotokos. In a miraculous way, she gave birth to Jesus Christ, the Son of God.

Jesus walked the earth, preaching, healing, and raising the dead. However, people with dark, hardened hearts were envious of Him and couldn't bear the light that came from Him. They told lies about Him and sentenced Him to death.

(continued on the next page)

> Whoever eats my flesh and drinks my blood has eternal life, and I will raise him up on the last day. For my flesh is true food, and my blood is true drink. Whoever feeds on my flesh and drinks my blood abides in me, and I in him.
>
> **The Gospel of John, Chapter 6, Verses 53–56**

The Theotokos

Pay attention to how many icons there are in Church of the Virgin Mary, holding in her arms her Son, the Infant Christ. We praise her and call her the Theotokos and the Mother of God and we ask her always to hear us, comfort us, and support us through her prayers.

The night before His arrest, the Lord Jesus Christ, knowing that they would soon seize Him, took bread, broke it, and gave it to His disciples, saying, "This is My Body, which is given for you. Do this in remembrance of Me."

Then, He took a cup of wine. "This cup is the New Testament in My Blood, which is shed for you!" He said, giving the cup to the disciples.

That was how the first Liturgy took place. We call it the Mystical Supper.

Jesus was killed by crucifixion on the Cross. But He is the God-man and so death was unable to hold Him. Three days later, Christ rose from the dead. The day of His resurrection changed the whole world. The way into the Kingdom of Heaven was opened to all mankind. Sunday, the day He rose from the dead, came to be known as the Day of Resurrection and that is why every Sunday, we gather to celebrate Liturgy.

> **For almost two thousand years,** through a divine miracle, the bread and wine brought to Liturgy become the Body and Blood of Jesus Christ. While in appearance the Holy Gifts still look like wine and bread, when we taste them we are joined with the Risen Christ. He enters into our hearts and we partake in immortality.

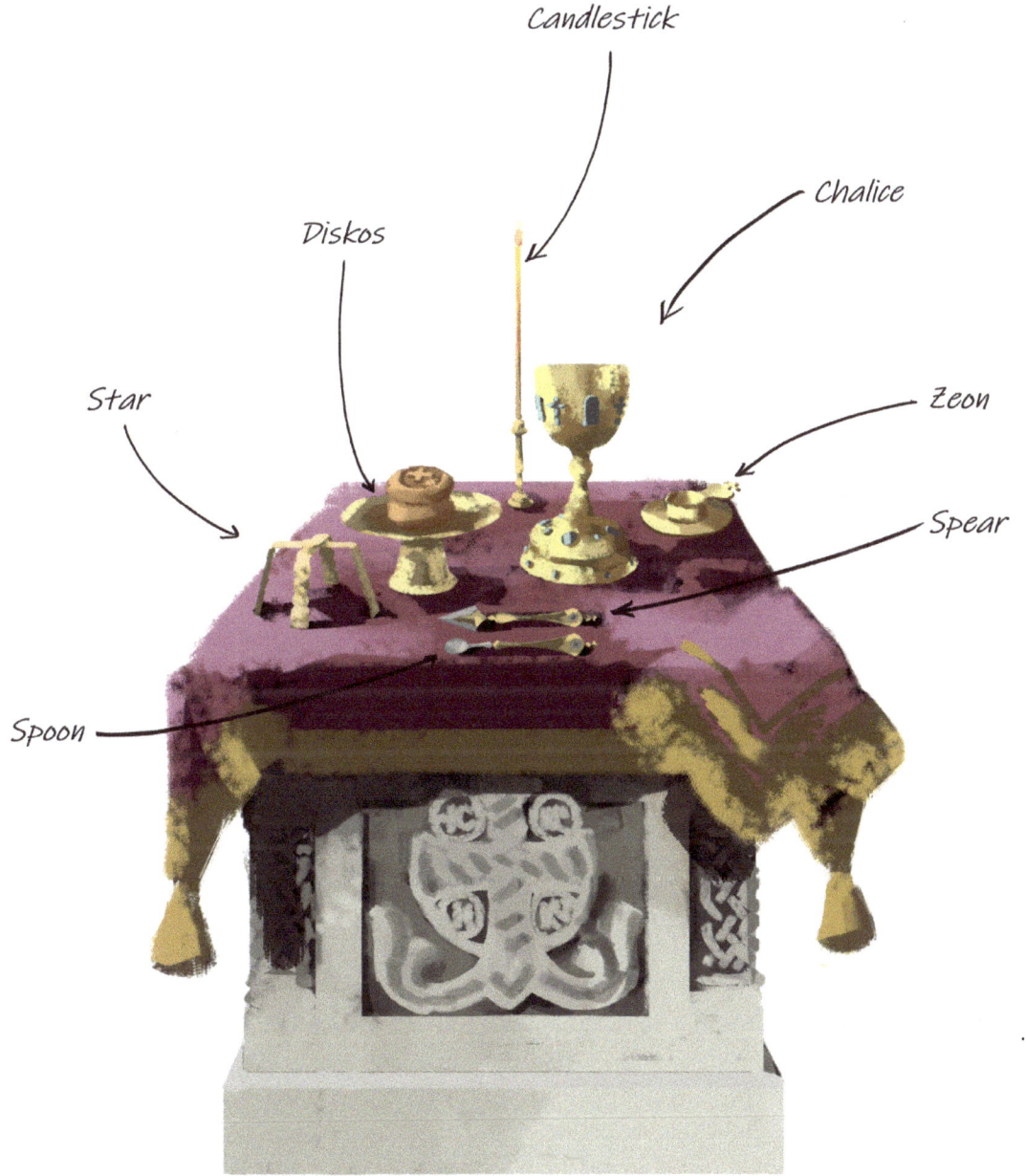

The Prothesis Table

PREPARATION

The Liturgy begins with preparation. Everything necessary is brought into the Altar – first and foremost, the bread and wine. The wine has to be natural wine, made from grapes, and the bread has to be made from wheat and be fresh and tasty. Often, the bread for Liturgy is baked at the Church itself. It is called "prosphora" which means "offering."

In ancient times, the bread was always prepared by the people. They brought it, along with their own wine. They offered the best that they had. The offerings were put on a special table called the "prothesis." For Liturgy, the clergy selected the best from what had been offered. Everything that was left was blessed after the service and distributed as part of a common meal. The poor were always invited to the meal since they didn't have anything to call their own.

(continued on the next page)

The Altar

The Altar is the most important place in the temple. Only the clergy, and those who assist them, can enter. The Altar is hidden behind the iconostasis. In the center of the Altar is the Holy Table. It is on the Holy Table that the greatest wonder in the world takes place. It is here that the bread and wine become the Body and Blood of Jesus Christ.

The Divine Liturgy

As the priest enters the Altar, he asks for God's blessing to serve Liturgy. Then, he prays as he puts on each piece of his vestments. Liturgy is above all a thing of joy and the holy vestments represent the joy and righteousness of the Kingdom of God.

The priest takes the bread and prayerfully commemorates the sufferings of Christ as he places a large square section of the bread – the Lamb – on a special tray called the Diskos. He pours the wine into a beautiful Chalice. When Jesus was suffering on the cross, one of the Roman soldiers pierced His side with a spear. Blood and water flowed out of the wound. In memory of that, a little bit of water is added to the Chalice.

Besides the big prosphora loaf, other loaves are prepared as well, often a little smaller. The people write lists with the names of their loved ones. Those lists are brought into the Altar where the priest prays for each one of them. In his hand, he has a small knife, called the "Spear," that he deftly uses to take out a small particle from the other loaves of prosphora for each name. Then, he carefully places the particles on the Diskos near the Lamb which was taken from the big prosphora loaf and which will become the Body of Christ. Each particle represents a specific person that the priest prayed for. The rest of the loaves are cut up and given to the people at the end of Liturgy.

Love

Do you know what explains everything that we do during Liturgy? Well, think about what explains many of your other actions. For example, you feel something inside yourself, something important. It's strong love. So you hug your mom and dad and your feeling goes from the inside to the outside, to your actions. All of our actions during Liturgy are our love for God expressing itself. They show our desire to embrace God and His holiness.

The censer is lit. A censer is a beautiful metal bowl, hanging from chains. Inside, there is a piece of charcoal, glowing red, on which little pieces of sweet-smelling incense are placed. A pleasant, sweet smoke then rises from the censer, not at all like normal smoke. The priest or the deacon then uses the censer first to cense the altar and then the whole temple and all the icons.

Censing is also an expression of love for God, for the Theotokos and the saints, and for all people. The priest or deacon also censes each person standing there in the temple.

The bread and wine are left on the prothesis table. The preparation is finished.

IN THE KINGDOM OF GOD

It's time for us to prepare our hearts to receive God. All the candles in the Church are lit. The Royal Doors are opened. Liturgy begins.

The priest solemnly proclaims, "Blessed is the Kingdom of the Father and the Son and the Holy Spirit, now and ever and unto ages of ages. Amen." God is the Trinity, the Father, the Son, and the Holy Spirit.

Once, an elder with a pure heart saw an angel going around the Church and anointing people, but only those who were praying attentively, from their hearts. He also anointed a few empty places. The elder was surprised and asked the angel why he did that. "Those who through illness or for other good reasons couldn't come to Liturgy," the angel responded, "but who are still praying to God from their heart, receive the anointing of grace, too. In their hearts, they are here, in the Kingdom of God."

If, however, we fidget, are bored, and think about how soon it will all be over, then even if we are standing in the temple, it doesn't help us. The Kingdom of God passes us by.

The Kingdom of God

The Kingdom of God itself comes to us during Liturgy. In this Kingdom, the angels serve God with us.

The choir sings psalms and prayers, joyful hymns of the Kingdom of Christ. These hymns were sung hundreds and even a thousand years ago. Our ancestors in the faith sang them. Our great-great-great-great-grandfathers and grandmothers in the faith sang them. They also didn't understand all the words at first when they were small children. Those, however, who learned to see and hear with their hearts shared in God's joy and immortality. They are also in the temple with us, rejoicing with you, and talking to Christ and the Theotokos about you.

THE LITURGY AND THE WHOLE WORLD

God holds the whole world in His hands, so don't be afraid of anything. Fifteen hundred years ago, in the city of Constantinople, there was a great earthquake. The people were greatly afraid and gathered to ask God to save them from death. During this communal prayer, one brave boy was raised up to Heaven. There he saw the angels praising the greatness of God. When the earthquake was over, the boy came back and told the people about the angels' prayer that he had memorized. Ever since then, Christians have prayed in the way that the little boy taught them, singing that angelic prayer during the Divine Liturgy.

Throughout the whole Liturgy, the priest prays, standing in the Altar in front of the Holy Table, and the angels help him, invisibly. However, those who are able to see with their hearts will feel their presence.

The priest also has a visible helper: the deacon. Of course, not every parish has a deacon but when there is a deacon, the services are especially beautiful. The deacon wears a stikharion, a long, embroidered robe with wide sleeves and a long strip of fabric (called an "orarion") wrapped around his left shoulder. A long time

---

The Angelic Prayer

"Holy God, Holy Mighty, Holy Immortal, have mercy on us."

"Mighty" means that God is strong and all powerful. "Immortal" means that He is the source of life. We ask God's mercy for the whole world.

ago, in addition to helping the priest, the deacons supervised the children during Liturgy, taught them to pray, and explained to them what was happening in the temple building. The deacon frequently comes out of the Altar to call us all to prayer. With his right hand, he lifts up the orarion and it reminds us of an angel's wings.

Liturgy teaches us to love all people. The deacon calls on us to pray both for our own country and for all countries, so that all people might live in peace with each other. He calls us to pray for those who are sick, suffering, or languishing in prison. It's not good for us to ask God to meet only our own needs.

Orarion

Stikharion

THE HOLY GOSPEL

On the Holy Table, there is a book: the Holy Gospel, a sacred book that was written by the disciples of Jesus Christ. This book tells us about His miraculous birth, about everything that He said and did during His earthly life, about His suffering, death, Resurrection, and Ascension to God the Father in Heaven. Every Christian should have a copy of the Holy Gospels and read it every day.

From the priest's prayer before the Gospel:

"Illumine our hearts, O Master who lovest mankind, with the pure light of thy divine knowledge, and open our spiritual eyes to understand Thy gospel teachings..."

The copy of the Gospels used for the Divine Services is special. It lies on the Holy Table, reminding us that Christ is always with us. During Liturgy, the clergy carry the Gospel out of the Altar to read it to the people. During the Gospel reading, Jesus Christ Himself is speaking to each of us through the Gospel.

A lighted candle is brought out with the Gospel. Light overcomes darkness. Even a tiny flame. If you light a little candle in the darkness, things will get a little bit brighter. In the same way, every good deed you do, no matter how small, will change the world for the better. We need to remember that.

23 The Divine Liturgy

THE GREAT ENTRANCE

We're getting close to the heart of the Divine Liturgy. While we've been praying, the bread and wine have still been on the prothesis table. In order for them to be sanctified, they need to be brought, solemnly and triumphantly, to the place of God's power and glory, the Holy Table. That could be done simply, without even going out of the Altar. The Liturgy, however, is for all of us and it is important to Christ that we all fully participate in it.

First, the altar servers exit the Altar, carrying lanterns. Then, the clergy come out, carrying the Chalice and the Diskos, exiting through one of the side doors of the iconostasis, and coming around to stand in front of the middle of the iconostasis. After praying for us, they go through the Holy Doors into the Altar. The bread and wine are now on the Holy Table, waiting for the great Mystery that will soon come to pass.

The Cherubic Hymn

Let us who mystically represent the Cherubim and sing the thrice-holy hymn to the Life-creating Trinity now lay aside every earthly care that we may receive the King of all who comes invisibly escorted by the angelic hosts. Alleluia!

(For an explanation of this prayer, see page 32)

The Divine Liturgy

THE HEART OF LITURGY

Together, we all sing or say the Symbol of Faith, a creed in which we confess our Orthodox faith in God the Trinity.

Then, when the priest says the words, "Let us give thanks unto the Lord," the most important part of Liturgy begins. The heart of Liturgy, its foundation and soul, is the prayer of the Holy Apostles, which the Church has prayed over the bread and wine for two thousand years. The prayer begins with thanksgiving for the miracle of life: "Holy, holy, holy art Thou, Lord of Sabaoth, heaven and earth are full of Thy glory." When the angels sing this prayer, they cover their faces with their wings before the majesty of God and before the radiance coming from Him. Time itself disappears in that radiance.

After giving thanks, the prayer speaks of the Covenant that the Son of God left us. The prayer leads us into the Mystical Supper. The priest points at the bread and wine with his hand, saying the words that the Lord Himself said, "Take, eat, this is My Body," and "Drink of this, all of you, this is My Blood." We all respond by saying, "Amen," which means "so be it."

Having remembered the Lord's Covenant, the priest continues by raising his hands to heaven and asking God to accept our offering.

Then, a miracle takes place. The Holy Spirit descends on the bread and wine and sanctifies them, and they become the Body and Blood of Jesus Christ.

(continued on the next page)

The Divine Liturgy

The priest blesses the bread, making the sign of the cross over it while saying:
"And make this bread the precious Body of Thy Christ."

Then, he blesses the Chalice in the same way, saying:
"And that which is in this Cup, the precious Blood of Thy Christ."

Finally, he blesses them both, saying:
"Changing them by Thy Holy Spirit."

After this miracle, we all sing or say the "Our Father," the prayer that Christ Himself taught us.

Learn this prayer by heart. It is a simple prayer, yet the most beautiful. Reading it, each of us becomes the child of God, for in it we talk to God not as the great and awesome master of the world, but rather as our loving Heavenly Father.

Next, we come to the part of Liturgy that shows us the reason why the bread and wine became Christ's Body and Blood. It is time for us to receive Communion, to partake in the Holy Gifts. The Holy Doors are opened and the priest comes out with the Chalice in his hands. Using a special long Spoon, he places a small piece of the Body and Blood of Christ in the mouth of each person receiving Communion. We receive the Holy Gifts and Christ Himself enters our hearts,

Our Father, who art in heaven, hallowed be Thy Name, Thy kingdom come, Thy will be done, on earth as it is in heaven. Give us this day our daily bread. And forgive us our trespasses, as we forgive those who trespass against us. And lead us not into temptation, but deliver us from the evil one.

(For an explanation of this prayer, see page 32)

From the Prayers of Thanskgiving

May Thy holy Body, O Lord Jesus Christ my God, be to me for eternal life and Thy precious Blood be for the forgiveness of my sins. May this Eucharist be to me for joy, health, and gladness…

and we become immortal citizens of the Kingdom of God.

The ancient prophet Isaiah, seeing the glory of God, was afraid and wept, saying, "Woe is me! I am undone! For I am a man of unclean lips." The Lord told him, "Do not be afraid." At these words, an angel carrying tongs took a burning coal from the Altar and touched Isaiah's lips and said, "Behold, this has touched your lips and the Lord will take away all your transgressions and purge away your sins."

When we receive Communion, the Lord cleanses us from all of our sins.

THE LORD IS WAITING FOR YOU

We receive eternal life as a gift, but it is a gift that we must tend to within ourselves. After all, it's possible to get a gift you've wanted for a long time, for example a toy or a game, and break it or lose it that same day. If we're not careful, it can be just as easy to lose the gift of eternal life that Christ has given us.

Once some people brought their children to see Christ. There were a lot of children. They were playing and making noise. The disciples decided not to let these people with all their children see Jesus. They were afraid they'd cause chaos and were nervous that the children would bother Jesus with their games. Jesus, however, said, "Let the little children come to me and do not hinder them for the Kingdom of God is theirs!"

How, then, do we protect this gift? First of all, by not allowing bad desires into our hearts and by trying to do good. That means that you should treat others the way you want them to treat you. Jesus taught us that.

He also commanded us to forgive those who offend us. "If you forgive," Jesus said, "then your Heavenly Father will forgive you, too." Also, it's very important that you don't forget to ask forgiveness when you upset someone. Don't, however, pretend. Don't try to be good just so that other people will notice and praise you. Do good in simplicity of heart, since Christ doesn't like it when we only pretend to be good.

On Sunday morning, get dressed, wash your face, and go with joy! The Kingdom of Heaven is yours! The Lord loves you and that is why you are going to Liturgy on Sunday. He is waiting for you.

The Divine Liturgy

AN EXPLANATION OF TWO IMPORTANT PRAYERS

The Cherubic Hymn

Let us who mystically represent the Cherubim and sing the thrice-holy hymn to the Life-creating Trinity now lay aside every earthly care that we may receive the King of all who comes invisibly escorted by the angelic hosts. Alleluia!

During Liturgy, we join in the worship that the angels constantly offer to God. We enter into eternity and together with the Cherubim, praise and sing to God, the Holy Trinity. But in order for us to offer Him pure worship, we need to leave our worries behind and think only about Him.

The Lord's Prayer

Our Father, who art in heaven, hallowed be Thy Name, Thy kingdom come, Thy will be done, on earth as it is in heaven. Give us this day our daily bread. And forgive us our trespasses, as we forgive those who trespass against us. And lead us not into temptation, but deliver us from the evil one.

When the disciples asked Christ to teach them to pray, He taught them this prayer. This short, simple prayer shows us many things. First, it shows us that God is our true Father. Then, it shows us how important it is for us to wish for the coming of God's Kingdom. It also shows us that we should always try to do God's will and that He is the one who gives us everything we need. It teaches us that if we want God to forgive us, we should also forgive other people. Finally, it shows us that when we're tempted by sin, we should turn to God, who is always there to help us.

www.ingramcontent.com/pod-product-compliance
Lightning Source LLC
Chambersburg PA
CBHW042354280426
43661CB00095B/1046